Midnight Riders

A Fun Song About the Ride of Paul Revere and William Dawes

By Michael Dahl

Illustrated by Brandon Reibeling

Special thanks to our advisers for their expertise:

Tom Mega, Ph.D., Department of History
University of St. Thomas (Minnesota)

Susan Kesselring, M.A., Literacy Educator
Rosemount–Apple Valley–Eagan (Minnesota) School District

PICTURE WINDOW BOOKS
MINNEAPOLIS, MINNESOTA

Managing Editor: Bob Temple
Creative Director: Terri Foley
Editor: Kristin Thoennes Keller
Editorial Adviser: Andrea Cascardi
Copy Editor: Laurie Kahn
Musical arrangement: Elizabeth Temple
Designer: Melissa Voda
Page production: The Design Lab
The illustrations in this book were created digitally.

Picture Window Books

**5115 Excelsior Boulevard
Suite 232
Minneapolis, MN 55416
1-877-845-8392
www.picturewindowbooks.com**

Library of Congress Cataloging-in-Publication Data
Dahl, Michael.
Midnight riders : a fun song about the ride of Paul Revere and William Dawes / author, Michael Dahl ;
illustrator, Brandon Reibeling.
p. cm. — (Fun songs)
Summary: Relates the Revolutionary War adventures of Paul Revere and William Dawes, who alerted the
minutemen when British troops arrived in Boston, interspersed with verses of original song lyrics to be
sung to the tune of "Over Hill, Over Dale." Includes bibliographical references (p.) and index.
ISBN 1-4048-0129-4
1. Revere, Paul, 1735-1818—Juvenile literature. 2. Dawes, William, 1745-1799—Juvenile literature.
3. Massachusetts—History—Revolution, 1775-1783—Juvenile literature. 4. Revere, Paul, 1735-1818—Songs
and music—Juvenile literature. 5. Dawes, William, 1745-1799—Songs and music—Juvenile literature.
6. Massachusetts—History—Revolution, 1775-1783—Songs and music—Juvenile literature. [1. Revere, Paul,
1735-1818. 2. Dawes, William, 1745-1799. 3. Massachusetts—History—Revolution—1775-1783. 4. Revere,
Paul, 1735-1818—Songs and music. 5. Dawes, William, 1745-1799—Songs and music. 6. Massachusetts—
History—Revolution—1775-1783—Songs and music.]
I. Reibeling, Brandon, ill. II. Title.
F69.R43 D34 2003
973.3'311'0922—dc21   200300983

SING ONE! SING ALL!
It's the new historical ditty:
"Midnight Riders."

Sing along to the tune of "Over Hill, Over Dale."
Tell the tale of fearless riders Paul Revere and William Dawes.
They risked their lives for freedom!

Long ago, people who lived in America were called colonists. The King of Great Britain ruled these people. He made them pay money to him. Many people did not think these taxes were fair. They got tired of being part of Britain. They called themselves patriots and fought the king's troops for their freedom.

On April 18, 1775, a British general made a plan. He knew the patriots had some weapons and gunpowder. They were hidden in a town called Concord. The general wanted to take those supplies. He planned to lead his men there. First, he had to make sure no one would leave Boston. He did not want the patriots in Concord to know his plan. He made the people of Boston stay in the city. He warned that his troops would shoot people who tried to leave.

How would the Boston patriots warn their friends in Concord? Two men offered to make the trip. They were Paul Revere and William Dawes. These brave men left the city on horseback. Both rode toward Lexington. This town was on the way to Concord. Patriot leaders were in Lexington. They had to be warned. This song tells the story of that night.

Up the hill,
down the trail,

4

see those rockets with a tail!

Paul and Will race their horses tonight!

The two riders did not take the same path. They hoped one of them would get the warning out.

Rushing 'round Charlestown, nothing slows Paul Revere down.

Paul and Will race their horses tonight!

"Hey, rise up and run
on the road to Lexington!

The British are landing on the shore!"

Paul saw two lanterns in a Boston church tower. This was a signal from another patriot. It meant the British were rowing across the Charles River instead of leaving Boston by land.

At each door they shout,
and the minutemen rush out.

Paul and Will race their horses tonight!

The minutemen were patriots.
They could be ready to fight
in one minute's time.

13

Pull up, Paul!
Slow down, Will!
See those redcoats
round that hill!

British soldiers are marching tonight!

Revere's route
Dawes's route
British route

Lexington

Menotomy

Medford

Cambridge

Charleston

Roxbury

Boston

British troops guarded the roads. They stopped anyone trying to pass. The patriots called them redcoats because of their bright red jackets.

Will escapes!
Paul is caught
but without
a single shot!

British soldiers
are marching
tonight!

British troops captured both riders. William escaped. Paul was released without his horse and walked to Lexington. He got there in time to see the end of the battle.

Paul tells whopping lies,
fills the soldiers with surprise:

"We have hundreds of men
just out of sight!"

Paul did not know how many patriots would fight. At Concord, however, British troops did find hundreds of patriots. The two sides fought for several hours before the British gave up.

19

So the redcoats run.
Paul and Will's good work is done.

Paul and Will saved the patriots last night!

Without Paul and Will, the patriots would have been hit hard. The British could have taken their supplies. They could have killed the patriot leaders. Paul and Will were heroes.

Midnight Riders

Up the hill, down the trail, see those rock–ets with a tail! Paul and Will race their hor–ses to–

night!   Rush–ing 'round Char–les–town, no–thing slows Paul Re–vere down. Paul and

Will race their hor–ses to–night! Hey, rise up and run on the road to Lex–ing–ton! The

Brit–ish are land–ing on the shore!   At each door they   shout,   and the

min–ute–men rush out. Paul and Will   race their hor–ses to–night!

2. Pull up, Paul! Slow down, Will!
   See those redcoats round that hill!
   British soldiers are marching tonight!
   Will escapes! Paul is caught
   But without a single shot!
   British soldiers are marching tonight!

   Paul tells whopping lies, fills the soldiers with surprise:
   We have hundreds of men just out of sight!
   So the redcoats run. Paul and Will's good work is done.
   Paul and Will saved the patriots last night!

Did You Know?

Did you know about Sybil Ludington?
Sybil risked her life to warn patriots, just like Paul and Will.
But she was only 16 years old!

On April 26, 1777, someone knocked on the door at Sybil's house. He brought scary news. The British were burning the nearby town of Danbury, Connecticut. Someone had to stop them. Sybil rode her horse 40 miles toward the town. She knocked on doors and banged on windows.

Sybil woke up enough people to join the patriots. The town was on fire when they arrived. The British troops did not expect these fighters and gave up fighting. But the town was already ruined.

Did you know about Samuel Prescott?
He was a doctor who also rode on that famous night. Samuel met up with Paul and William as they rode out of Lexington. He knew the area well. Samuel was captured by the British but escaped right away.

GLOSSARY

colonist—a person who lives in a new land but is ruled by people in a former land

lantern—a light or candle with a frame to protect it

minutemen—soldiers who could be ready to fight in one minute

patriot—a person who loves and fights for his or her country

row—to use oars to move a boat through water

tax—money that people pay to their government

23

To Learn More

AT THE LIBRARY

Barner, Bob. *Which Way to the Revolution?: A Book About Maps.* New York: Holiday House, 1998.

Fritz, Jean. *And Then What Happened, Paul Revere?* New York: PaperStar, 1996.

Krensky, Stephen. *Paul Revere's Midnight Ride.* New York: HarperCollins, 2002.

ON THE WEB

National Museum of American History

http://www.americanhistory.si.edu

Tells stories from American history and includes hands-on activities

The Paul Revere House

http://www.paulreverehouse.org

Shows Paul's house and tells his story

Fact Hound

Fact Hound offers a safe, fun way to find Web sites related to this book. All of the sites on Fact Hound have been researched by our staff.

http://www.facthound.com

1. Visit the Fact Hound home page.
2. Enter a search word related to this book or type in this special code: 1404801294.
3. Click on the FETCH IT button.

Your trusty Fact Hound will fetch the best sites for you!